THE POMEGRANATE SONGS

Rina Youngblood

Presentation by *BookLeaf Publishing*

Web: www.bookleafpub.com

E-mail: info@bookleafpub.com

ISBN : 9789357445559

First edition 2022

MY NAME

Don't call me by my name. A name my mother wove for me with her coarse hands, cracked and red from the harvest. A name with summer in the weft, a name that loves the heat the way a flame loves the tinder grass of a baked brown valley. A name for the sear of lightning, the clouds of warm rain, a name for breaking river banks. A name bright with the songs of cicadas, the shine of their still wet wings, like slices of sun on a lake where the swans call out amongst the reed-mace. A name laced with the ripples of their unseen passage. You would not know the pattern.

YOURS

I say your name and it is a curse. It is a lungful of ice,
a name of cold desire, a name of mud and silt. A name
too dark
to look upon, too sharp for mortals, they avert their eyes,
unable
to bear the knife edge of those syllables against their
gaze. The flimsy
creatures weep tears of blood and you lap them up. You
see me
watching and I do not need to say that you are all
together too
much animal, all reflex and instinct, grinding muscle.
Slippery and taut, coils of snake. I say your name
and revel in the sound of it. It tastes like cheap wine on
my
tongue, more sour with every breath. It sticks like gristle
between
my teeth. I smile and it gleams greasy on my lips. Wipe
it off
with the back of my hand. I'll waste your name, lover.
There is laughter in the joke I make of it, poison mirth.
Such a sweet cocktail, pleasure and scorn.

STYX

Take me to the black river where the water sings its
ancient song
of skinned bones and plague. To the shores of ash, your
hand in mine,
your touch a keen ache, a bare-toothed winter. The trees
are bare
and shivering. I shed my dress, I stand bare and
shivering,
I press the prints of my feet into the silt until they meet
the water.
Cold as crushed glass; was that your design? The glacial
song,
the way the horizon cuts the sky, flat as satyr's eyes,
the sting of the tide on my skin. It tastes like a widow's
tears,
a mother's wail, the waves wash up in agonal gasps.
It tastes of drowning, a lungful of ice, bubbles of prayer,
of vacant rooms. Bullets and butterfly knives.
At the door, the hungry dogs loiter and slaver.
Waist-deep now, someone is screaming to the gods,
their hands are pink and thrashing like blind piglets.
In that voice a slaughterhouse shriek, in that shriek
a silhouette shape in the weeds, the crabgrass will eat
them.
Look now, the skin of them is dead and pale,
but their eyes are alive with worms.
There's a cry: darling, how could you, please stop.

The river is lapping your feet behind me, and I wonder
how one so beautiful could shape something so cruel.
Darling, I almost say, darling, how could you.
Darling, I almost say, but instead I sink down
and let the river swallow me whole.

CREATURE FEAR

I close my eyes and see the dogs running,
snarling and tossing, eyes rolling, gleaming like pearls.
I can hear them thrashing through the trees,
the shallows of the river, their howls chasing them down
past the cairns and temples, the descending clouds.
I open my hand and there is a stone in it,
the colour of a wolf's heart. You're standing in the yard,
looking at the belly of the sky, you threw your heart
down a well and it hasn't hit the bottom yet.
There is no sound unholier than the cry of a dog
with its legs cut out from under it, but it's echoing
down the halls and boulevardes, screaming, yelping.
I touch my belly and think of ghouls and fledglings.
I open my eyes and hear a stone strike water.

SOFTLY

Come on, my love. Clench the barbed wire in your fist.
Bite down
on the razor. The bear trap is set, the teeth await your
flesh. But no;
I see the fear in you. I hear it in you when you call me
dear, precious.
In the dark you say darling and I let it slip away, cheroot
smoke.
When you think I am asleep you say oh love, even then
you do not
dare to call me yours. But the temptation is there in the
thick black
cords of your voice. You think my name is a bird to be
captured,
sparrow quick, osprey fierce. You watch its flight, its
shadow,
you were too busy looking at its yellow eyes
that you forgot to listen to its song.

WHITE HEAT

One day you will dare to speak the sound of my name.
You will think of Prometheus and his gift of fire,
the sprig of fennel, the light that burned the wide-eyed
men,
their crude hasty hands, their wet mouths,
slavering in their lust for cooked meat.
Falling upon the blackened fur, the dripping flesh.
You think you will learn something of that,
you expect my name to blister upon your lips and
scorch a ragged scar across your tongue.
Wildfire name, volcano name, coal hot.
Embers in a palm. Swallow them down.
It'll split you like lightning wracks the sky above a hill,
whip crack, a god's finger lanced into the grass,
so dry and full of sweet summer heat.
Don't look now, but the fields are afire.
The horses are running and choking,
ash in their lungs, ash clouding their hooves
as they run themselves into the river.
The foxes are running and tearing at the smoke,
perhaps you'll run too, melting, scrambling
as the fire turns your teeth to alabaster.
In the pits of your eyes yawns a flame.
Take a deep breath. Blink. Let me see the fear between
your lashes.

BESIDE ME

Your eyes are open
but slowly shuttering
I think of windows
of a house in the woods
the sunlight falling on floorboards
and wisteria slowly tearing
the gutter from the roof
casting velvet shadows
where you would not hold me
your hands painted gold
cupping my jaw
and touching the bone
through my cheek.

A stupid dream. Go to sleep.

SALTED

No one told me that gold
would taste like this
until a man with no legs
drew me a map
crude lines, dry parchment
the path to a crumbling cove
where the teeth of sprites
glow like pearls
dripping with nacre
there I collected jawbones
by the dozen
placed them in a sack
sold them to naiads
a coin per tooth
(do you know their slippery skin
the scales on their tongues
the whiteness of their meat?
if anyone knew, it would be you)
I left them with gold
heavy in my pockets
Behind me I heard
their clawed fingers scrape
across each tooth and groove
whispering prayers
remembering names.

DESIRE

Don't look at me like that.
Soon I'll gouge into those eyes
bright, gelatinous.
Scrape the backs of the sockets.
Unpick your skin with a buck knife
to expose the fat nestled amongst
those slim working muscles.
Cartilage gleaming amongst the viscera.
I'll reach elbow deep between broken ribs
to heft out each steaming organ
and kiss every raw piece of you.

SMOKE

Smoke will linger
if you do not stir
taste it in silence
coal hot, balefire bright
candle flicker, match sharp
shut your eyes to the sting
suspire, asphixiate
winnowing breath
raise a hand and watch
the smoke disperse
leaving only bitter perfume
as dark swallows flame.

ONE DAY

In a valley far away, an orchard
of brambles and blackberries, heavy
on thorned and hungry vines
that know not mortal hands
only the rains of summer's end
and the white fires of gods

Amongst them an ancient tree
limbs in full fruit, swollen and straining
to burst through speckled skins
moist and blooded as flesh
translucent and throbbing
with living shadows of seeds

Beneath that tree, buried roots
thrust through crawling soil
rich with beetles and clay
They'll never bury us, darling
No soft dark earth to hold us
or worms for our eyes

Only the whisper through boughs
carried without breeze
wrought from prayer and curse
a chorus of our names
a rising river on cold stones.

UNBIDDEN

Far from you but not far enough
to escape the cant of your head
the angle of your shoulders
carved into every stone
drawing my eye like a lodestone
in false and treacherous hope.

I do not speak your name
not for fear of its sound
but for fear of its taste.

TIDES

Upon a ship upon the river
The breath of wind in your hair
Somewhere, a litany of hazy songs
Your shadow gliding across the water
Mine rippling beside it
I imagine it raising a hand
to lay against the black of your cheek
Would it feel the bone of your skull
through your skin?
Would it feel the candleflame
in the murk of your undying heart?

Softly, now.

ULTRAVIOLET

Your gaze burns. Your hands are hard as they hold me
and I know they will leave bruises, bright as warpaint.
My hands are fists and I want to pound a drumbeat into
your chest. You hold me but you don't hold me to you.
The sunlight falls over us. The distant starlight falls over
us. Remote galactic fires that cast your face in sharp
relief. That set the bitter dark of your pupils alight. Our
shadows are collisions on the ground, absorbing into the
asphalt. I am saying words, so many words, but you
cannot hear them. I am saying incantations, spells, to
root you here in this place. Be my Atlas, you fool. Stay,
the way you had stayed splayed across the bed on dim
mornings before daybreak, before the light had come
through the window slats. Tell me you remember the
quietness of the air and the warmth between our bodies,
languid and sticky from leftover dreams. You were a
silhouette, a smoky blur against a deeper darkness. Tell
me you remember these cooling memories. It's so cold
in this strange light now. Tell me you remember. And let
me in and carve you open, because it's cold, because
inside you there is a fire and I want to eat the embers by
the handfuls.

FEAST

You fished ice cubes from your glass
and swallowed them whole
clinking against clenched teeth

My own belly empty
I wondered if you would choke
when once I would have hoped

I think of putting my hands
about your working throat
and wringing you out

but you would only drip
all over my fingers
and into the cutting night.

GHOSTS

Let us play a game, you and I
where your hands are hard and cracked
from wielding sickle and shovel
nails broken, half-mooned with dirt
but your skin is warm to my touch
your heart a beating beast
driving blood alive and coiling
through every vein, every artery

where each time I say your name
it tastes new and raw again
like fresh birch sap, crushed saffron
and the sound of mine in your mouth
springs brilliant into the air
from between your teeth
like the first fish of the season
breaking through lake ice.

You, warm beneath my hands
your name on my tongue
hot and heavy as curses
darker than our shadows
splayed across the clay wall
pressing into each other
darker than wildfire smoke
strange ghosts, we.

INFINITUM

In another world
a dappled dawn wood
where cicadas sing summer songs
my hand peeling empty exuvia from a tree
your footfalls on the soft worn path
a barefoot passage marked only
by crushed leaves

the bead of sweat upon your sunburnt brow
the fine movement of your brown limbs
pulled by muscle beneath skin
and in your heat shimmer wake
breathed in the memory
of your salt-spice smell.

In the dip of my palm,
a desiccated husk.

TRANSGRESSIONS

The mouth says hello, too soft, hoarse. The hands say
fear.
The heat beneath skin says desire. Tight in the chest,
the heart sings: mistake.
Then the hands lift like new birds
and commit their sins and errors.
I'll trade you my forgiveness for yours.